COMMENTS ON THE SOCIETY OF THE SPECTACLE

COMMENTS ON THE SOCIETY OF THE SPECTACLE

GUY DEBORD

VERSO

London • New York

This edition first published by Verso 1998
© Verso 1998
Translation © Malcolm Imrie 1990
First published as *Commentaires sur la société du spectacle*
© Édition Gérard Lébovici 1988

5 7 9 10 8 6 4

Verso
UK: 6 Meard Street, London W1F 0EG
US: 20 Jay Street, Suite 1010, Brooklyn, NY 11201
www.versobooks.com

Verso is the imprint of New Left Books

ISBN-13: 978-1-84467-672-9

British Library Cataloguing in Publication Data
A catalogue record for this book is available from the British Library

Library of Congress Cataloging-in-Publication Data
A catalog record for this book is available from the Library of Congress

Typeset by Hewer Text UK Ltd, Edinburgh
Printed by in the USA

In memory of Gérard Lebovici,
ambushed and murdered in Paris on
5 March 1984 by persons still unknown

However desperate the situation and circumstances, do not despair. When there is everything to fear, be unafraid. When surrounded by dangers, fear none of them. When without resources, depend on resourcefulness. When surprised, take the enemy itself by surprise.

SUN TZU, *The Art of War*

I

THESE *Comments* are sure to be welcomed by fifty or
sixty people; a large number given the times in which
we live and the gravity of the matters under discussion. But then, of course, in some circles I am
considered to be an authority. It must also be borne in
mind that a good half of this interested elite will
consist of people who devote themselves to maintaining the spectacular system of domination, and the
other half of people who persist in doing quite the
opposite. Having, then, to take account of readers who
are both attentive and diversely influential, I obviously cannot speak with complete freedom. Above all,
I must take care not to give too much information to
just anybody.

Our unfortunate times thus compel me, once again, to write in a new way. Some elements will be intentionally omitted; and the plan will have to remain rather unclear. Readers will encounter certain decoys, like the very hallmark of the era. As long as certain pages are interpolated here and there, the overall meaning may appear: just as secret clauses have very often been added to whatever treaties may openly stipulate; just as some chemical agents only reveal their hidden properties when they are combined with others. However, in this brief work there will be only too many things which are, alas, easy to understand.

II

IN 1967, in a book entitled *The Society of the Spectacle*, I showed what the modern spectacle was already in essence: the autocratic reign of the market economy which had acceded to an irresponsible sovereignty, and the totality of new techniques of government which accompanied this reign. The disturbances of 1968, which in several countries lasted into the following years, having nowhere overthrown the existing organisation of the society from which it springs apparently spontaneously, the spectacle has thus continued to gather strength; that is, to spread to the furthest limits on all sides, while increasing its density in the centre. It has even learnt new defensive techniques, as powers under attack always do. When I began the critique of spectacular society, what was particularly noticed – given the period – was the revolutionary content that could be discovered in that critique; and it was naturally felt to be its most troublesome element. As to the spectacle itself, I was sometimes accused of having invented it out of thin air, and was always accused of indulging myself to excess in my evaluation of its depth and unity, and its real workings. I must admit that others who later published new books on the same subject demonstrated that it was quite possible to say less. All they had to do was to replace the totality and its movement by a single static detail on the surface of the phenomenon, with each author demonstrating his originality by choosing a different and all the less disturbing one. No one wanted to taint the scientific modesty of his personal interpretation by interposing reckless historical judgements.

Nonetheless, the society of the spectacle has continued to advance. It moves quickly for in 1967 it had barely forty years behind it; though it had used them to the full. And by its own development, which no one took the trouble to investigate, it has since shown with some astonishing achievements that it was effectively just what I said it was. Proving this point has more than academic value, because it is undoubtedly indispensable to have understood the spectacle's unity and articulation as an active force in order to examine the directions in which this force has since been able to travel. These questions are of great interest, for it is under such conditions that the next stage of social conflict will necessarily be played out. Since the spectacle today is certainly more powerful than it was before, what is it doing with this additional power? What point has it reached, that it had not reached previously? What, in short, are its present *lines of advance*? The vague feeling that there has been a rapid invasion which has forced people to lead their lives in an entirely different way is now widespread; but this is experienced rather like some inexplicable change in the climate, or in some other natural equilibrium, a change faced with which ignorance knows only that it has nothing to say. What is more, many see it as a civilising invasion, as something inevitable, and even want to collaborate. Such people would rather not know the precise purpose of this conquest, and how it is advancing.

I am going to outline certain *practical consequences*, still little known, of the spectacle's rapid extension over the last twenty years. I have no intention of entering into polemics on any aspect of this question; these are now too easy, and too useless. Nor will I try to convince. The present comments are not concerned with moralising. They do not propose what is desirable, or merely preferable. They simply record what is.

III

NO ONE today can reasonably doubt the existence or the power of the spectacle; on the contrary, one might doubt whether it is reasonable to add anything on a question which experience has already settled in such draconian fashion. *Le Monde* of 19 September 1987 offered a felicitous illustration of the saying, 'If it exists, there's no need to talk about it', a fundamental law in these spectacular times which, at least in this respect, ensure there is no such thing as a backward country:

> That modern society is a society of the spectacle now goes without saying. Indeed people will soon only be conspicuous by their reticence. One loses count of all the books describing a phenomenon which now marks all the industrialised nations yet equally spares none of the countries which has still to catch up. What is so droll, however, is that all the books which do analyse this phenomenon, usually to deplore it, cannot but join the spectacle if they're to get attention.

It is true that this spectacular critique of the spectacle, which is not only late but, even worse, seeks 'attention' on the same level, inevitably sticks to vain generalities or hypocritical regrets; just as futile as the clowns who parade their well-mannered disillusion in newspapers.

The empty debate on the spectacle – that is, on the activities of the world's owners – is thus organised by the spectacle itself: everything is said about the extensive means at its disposal, to ensure that nothing is said about their extensive deployment. Rather than talk of the spectacle, people often prefer to use the term 'media'. And by this they mean to describe a mere instrument, a kind of public service which with impartial 'professionalism' would facilitate the new wealth of mass communication through mass media – a form of communication which has at last attained a unilateral purity, whereby decisions already taken are presented for passive admiration. For what is communicated are *orders*; and with perfect harmony, those who give them are also those who tell us what they think of them.

Spectacular power, which is so fundamentally unitary, so concentrated by the very weight of things, and entirely despotic in spirit, frequently rails at the appearance in its realm of a spectacular politics, a spectacular justice, a spectacular medicine and all the other similarly surprising examples of 'media excess'. Thus the spectacle would be merely the excesses of the media, whose nature, unquestionably good since it facilitates communication, is sometimes driven to extremes.

Often enough society's bosses declare themselves ill-served by their media employees: more often they blame the spectators for the common, almost bestial manner in which they indulge in the media's delights. A virtually infinite number of supposed differences within the media thus serve to screen what is in fact the result of a spectacular convergence, pursued with remarkable tenacity. Just as the logic of the commodity reigns over capitalists' competing ambitions, and the logic of war always dominates the frequent modifications in weaponry, so the harsh logic of the spectacle controls the abundant diversity of media extravagances.

In all that has happened in the last twenty years, the most important change lies in the very continuity of the spectacle. This has nothing to do with the perfecting of its media instruments, which had already reached a highly advanced stage of development: it means quite simply that the spectacle's domination has succeeded in raising a whole generation moulded to its laws. The extraordinary new conditions in which this entire generation has effectively lived constitute a precise and comprehensive summary of all that, henceforth, the spectacle will forbid; and also all that it will permit.

IV

ON a theoretical level I only need add a single detail to my earlier formulations, albeit one which has far-reaching consequences. In 1967 I distinguished two rival and successive forms of spectacular power, the concentrated and the diffuse. Both of them floated above real society, as its goal and its lie. The former, favouring the ideology condensed around a dictatorial personality, had accomplished the totalitarian counter-revolution, fascist as well as Stalinist. The latter, driving wage-earners to apply their freedom of choice to the vast range of new commodities now on offer, had represented the Americanisation of the world, a process which in some respects frightened but also successfully seduced those countries where it had been possible to maintain traditional forms of bourgeois democracy. Since then a third form has been established, through the rational combination of these two, and on the basis of a general victory of the form which had showed itself stronger: the diffuse. This is the *integrated spectacle*, which has since tended to impose itself globally.

Whereas Russia and Germany were largely responsible for the formation of the concentrated spectacle, and the United States for the diffuse form, the integrated spectacle has been pioneered by France and Italy. The emergence of this new form is attributable to a number of shared historical features, namely, the important role of the Stalinist party and unions in political and intellectual life, a weak democratic tradition, the long monopoly of power enjoyed by a single party of government, and the need to eliminate an unexpected upsurge in revolutionary activity.

The integrated spectacle shows itself to be simultaneously concentrated and diffuse, and ever since the fruitful union of the two has learnt to employ both these qualities on a grander scale. Their former mode of application has changed considerably. As regards concentration, the controlling centre has now become occult: never to be occupied by a known leader, or clear ideology. And on the diffuse side, the spectacle has never before put its mark to such a degree on almost the full range of socially produced behaviour and objects. For the final sense of the integrated spectacle is this – that it has integrated itself into reality to the same extent as it was describing it, and that it was reconstructing it as it was describing it. As a result, this reality no longer confronts the integrated spectacle as something alien. When the spectacle was concentrated, the greater part of surrounding society escaped it; when diffuse, a small part; today, no part. The spectacle has spread itself to the point where it now permeates all reality. It was easy to predict in theory what has been quickly and universally demonstrated by practical experience of economic reason's relentless accomplishments: that the globalisation of the false was also the falsification of the globe. Beyond a legacy of old books and old buildings, still of some significance but destined to continual reduction and, moreover, increasingly highlighted and classified to suit the spectacle's requirements, there remains nothing, in culture or in nature, which has not been transformed, and polluted, according to the means and interests of modern industry. Even genetics has become readily accessible to the dominant social forces.

Spectacular government, which now possesses all the means necessary to falsify the whole of production and perception, is the absolute master of memories just as it is the unfettered master of plans which will shape the most distant future. It reigns unchecked; *it executes its summary judgements.*

It is in these conditions that a parodic end of the division of labour suddenly appears, with carnivalesque gaiety; all the more welcome because it coincides with the generalised disappearance of all real ability. A financier can be a singer, a lawyer a police spy, a baker can parade his literary tastes, an actor can be president, a chef can philosophise on cookery techniques as if they were landmarks in universal history. Anyone can join the spectacle, in order publicly to adopt, or sometimes secretly practise, an entirely different activity from whatever specialism first made their name. Where 'media status' has acquired infinitely more importance than the value of anything one might actually be capable of doing, it is normal for this status to be readily transferable; for anyone, anywhere, to have the same right to the same kind of stardom. Most often these accelerated media particles pursue their own careers in the glow of statutorily guaranteed admiration. But it sometimes happens that the transition to the media provides the *cover* for several different enterprises, officially independent but in fact secretly linked by various ad hoc networks. With the result that occasionally the social division of labour, along with the readily foreseeable unity of its application, reappears in quite new forms: for example, one can now publish a novel in order to arrange an assassination. Such picturesque examples also go to show that one should never trust someone because of their job.

Yet the highest ambition of the integrated spectacle is still to turn secret agents into revolutionaries, and revolutionaries into secret agents.

V

THE society whose modernisation has reached the stage of the integrated spectacle is characterised by the combined effect of five principal features: incessant technological renewal; integration of state and economy; generalised secrecy; unanswerable lies; an eternal present.

Technological innovation has a long history, and is an essential component of capitalist society, sometimes described as industrial or post-industrial. But since its most recent acceleration (in the aftermath of the Second World War) it has greatly reinforced spectacular authority, by surrendering everybody to the mercy of specialists, to their calculations and to the judgements which always depend on them. The integration of state and economy is the most evident trend of the century; it is at the very least the motor of all recent economic developments. The defensive and offensive pact concluded between these two powers, economy and state, has provided them with the greatest common advantages in every field: each may be said to own the other; at any rate, it is absurd to oppose them, or to distinguish between their reasons and follies. This union, too, has proved to be highly favourable to the development of spectacular domination – indeed, the two have been indistinguishable from the very start. The other three features are direct effects of this domination, in its integrated stage.

Generalised secrecy stands behind the spectacle, as the decisive complement of all it displays and, in the last analysis, as its most vital operation.

The simple fact of being unanswerable has given

what is false an entirely new quality. At a stroke it is truth which has almost everywhere ceased to exist or, at best, has been reduced to the status of pure hypothesis. Unanswerable lies have succeeded in eliminating public opinion, which first lost the ability to make itself heard and then very quickly dissolved altogether. This evidently has significant consequences for politics, the applied sciences, the legal system and the arts.

The manufacture of a present where fashion itself, from clothes to music, has come to a halt, which wants to forget the past and no longer seems to believe in a future, is achieved by the ceaseless circularity of information, always returning to the same short list of trivialities, passionately proclaimed as major discoveries. Meanwhile news of what is genuinely important, of what is actually changing, comes rarely, and then in fits and starts. It always concerns this world's apparent condemnation of its own existence, the stages in its programmed self-destruction.

VI

SPECTACULAR domination's first priority was to eradicate historical knowledge in general; beginning with just about all rational information and commentary on the most recent past. The evidence for this is so glaring it hardly needs further explanation. With consummate skill the spectacle organises ignorance of what is about to happen and, immediately afterwards, the forgetting of whatever has nonetheless been understood. The more important something is, the more it is hidden. Nothing in the last twenty years has been so thoroughly coated in obedient lies as the history of May 1968. Some useful lessons have indeed been learnt from certain demystifying studies of those days; these, however, remain state secrets.

In France, it is some ten years now since a president of the republic, long ago forgotten but at the time still basking on the spectacle's surface, naively expressed his delight at 'knowing that henceforth we will live in a world without memory, where images flow and merge, like reflections on the water'. Convenient indeed for those in business, and who know how to stay there. The end of history gives power a welcome break. Success is guaranteed in all its undertakings, or at least the rumour of success.

How drastically any absolute power will suppress history depends on the extent of its imperious interests or obligations, and especially on its practical capacity to execute its aims. Ts'in Che Hoang Ti had books burned, but he never managed to get rid of all of them. In our own century Stalin went further, yet despite the various accomplices he managed to find outside his empire's borders, there remained a vast area of the world beyond the reach of his police, where his schemes could be ridiculed. With its new techniques now adopted globally, the integrated spectacle has done much better. Ineptitude compels universal respect; it is no longer permitted to laugh at it. In any case, it has become impossible to show that one is laughing.

History's domain was the memorable, the totality of events whose consequences would be lastingly apparent. And thus, inseparably, history was knowledge that should endure and aid in understanding, at least in part, what was to come: 'an everlasting possession', according to Thucydides. In this way history was the *measure* of genuine novelty. It is in the interests of those who sell novelty at any price to eradicate the means of measuring it. When social significance is attributed only to what is immediate, and to what will be immediate immediately afterwards, always replacing another, identical, immediacy, it can be seen that the uses of the media guarantee a kind of eternity of noisy insignificance.

The precious advantage which the spectacle has acquired through the *outlawing* of history, from having driven the recent past into hiding, and from having made everyone forget the spirit of history within society, is above all the ability to cover its own tracks – to conceal the very progress of its recent world conquest. Its power already seems familiar, as if it had always been there. All usurpers have shared this aim: to make us forget that *they have only just arrived.*

VII

WITH the destruction of history, contemporary events themselves retreat into a remote and fabulous realm of unverifiable stories, uncheckable statistics, unlikely explanations and untenable reasoning. For every imbecility presented by the spectacle, there are only the media's professionals to give an answer, with a few respectful rectifications or remonstrations. And they are hardly extravagant, even with these, for besides their extreme ignorance, their *personal and professional solidarity* with the spectacle's overall authority and the society it expresses makes it their duty, and their pleasure, never to diverge from that authority whose majesty must not be threatened. It must not be forgotten that every media professional is bound by wages and other rewards and recompenses to a master, and sometimes to several; and that every one of them knows he is dispensable.

All experts serve the state and the media and only in that way do they achieve their status. Every expert follows his master, for all former possibilities for independence have been gradually reduced to nil by present society's mode of organisation. The most useful expert, of course, is the one who can lie. With their different motives, those who need experts are falsifiers and fools. Whenever individuals lose the capacity to see things for themselves, the expert is there to offer an absolute reassurance. Once there were experts in Etruscan art, and competent ones, for Etruscan art was not for sale. But a period which, for example, finds it profitable to fake by chemical means various famous wines, can only sell them if it has created wine experts able to con connoisseurs into admiring their new, more distinctive, flavours. Cervantes remarks that 'under a poor cloak you commonly find a good drinker'. Someone who knows his wine may often understand nothing about the rules of the nuclear industry; but spectacular power calculates that if one expert can make a fool of him with nuclear energy, another can easily do the same with wine. And it is well known, for example, that media meteorologists, forecasting temperature or rainfall for the next forty-eight hours, are severely limited in what they say by the obligation to maintain certain economic, touristic and regional balances, when so many people make so many journeys on so many roads, between so many equally desolate places; thus they can only try to make their names as entertainers.

One aspect of the disappearance of all objective historical knowledge can be seen in the way that individual reputations have become malleable and alterable at will by those who control all information: information which is gathered and also – an entirely different matter – information which is broadcast. Their ability to falsify is thus unlimited. Historical evidence which the spectacle does not need to know ceases to be evidence. When the only fame is that bestowed by the grace and favour of a spectacular Court, disgrace may swiftly follow. An anti-spectacular notoriety has become something extremely rare. I myself am one of the last people to retain one, having never had any other. But it has also become extraordinarily suspect. Society has officially declared itself to be spectacular. To be known outside spectacular relations is already to be known as an enemy of society.

A person's past can be entirely rewritten, radically altered, recreated in the manner of the Moscow trials – and without even having to bother with anything as clumsy as a trial. Killing comes cheaper these days. Those who run the spectacle, or their friends, surely have no lack of false witnesses, though they may be unskilled – and how could the spectators who witness the exploits of these false witnesses ever recognise their blunders? – or false documents, which are always highly effective. Thus it is no longer possible to believe anything about anyone that you have not learned for yourself, directly. But in fact false accusations are rarely necessary. Once one controls the mechanism which operates the only form of social verification to be fully and universally recognised, one can say what one likes. The spectacle proves its arguments simply by going round in circles: by coming back to the start, by repetition, by constant reaffirmation in the only space left where anything can be publicly affirmed, and believed, precisely because that is the only thing to which everyone is witness. Spectacular power can similarly deny whatever it likes, once, or three times over, and change the subject; knowing full well there is no danger of any riposte, in its own space or any other.

For the agora, the general community, has gone, along with communities restricted to intermediary bodies or to independent institutions, to salons or cafés, or to workers in a single company. There is no place left where people can discuss the realities which concern them, because they can never lastingly free themselves from the crushing presence of media discourse and of the various forces organised to relay it. Nothing remains of the relatively independent judgement of those who once made up the world of learning; of those, for example, who used to base their self-respect on their ability to verify, to come close to an impartial history of facts, or at least to believe that such a history deserved to be known. There is no longer even any incontestable bibliographical truth, and the computerised catalogues of national libraries are well-equipped to remove any residual traces. It is disorienting to consider what it meant to be a judge, a doctor or a historian not so long ago, and to recall the obligations and imperatives they often accepted, within the limits of their competence: *men resemble their times more than their fathers.*

When the spectacle stops talking about something for three days, it is as if it did not exist. For it has then gone on to talk about something else, and it is that which henceforth, in short, exists. The practical consequences, as we see, are enormous.

We believe we know that in Greece history and democracy entered the world at the same time. We can prove that their disappearances have also been simultaneous.

To this list of the triumphs of power we should, however, add one result which has proved negative: once the running of a state involves a permanent and massive shortage of historical knowledge, that state can no longer be led strategically.

VIII

ONCE it attains the stage of the integrated spectacle, self-proclaimed democratic society seems to be generally accepted as the realisation of a *fragile perfection*. So that it must no longer be exposed to attacks, being fragile; and indeed is no longer open to attack, being perfect as no other society before it. It is a fragile society because it has great difficulty managing its dangerous technological expansion. But it is a perfect society for governing; and the proof is that all those who aspire to govern want to govern this one, in the same way, changing hardly a thing. For the first time in contemporary Europe no party or fraction of a party even tries to pretend that they wish to change anything significant. The commodity is beyond criticism: as a general system and even as the particular forms of junk which heads of industry choose to put on the market at any given time.

Wherever the spectacle has its dominion the only organised forces are those which want the spectacle. Thus no one can be the enemy of what exists, nor transgress the *omertà* which applies to everything. We have dispensed with that disturbing conception, which was dominant for over two hundred years, in which a society was open to criticism or transformation, reform or revolution. Not thanks to any new arguments, but quite simply because all argument has become useless. From this result we can estimate not universal happiness, but the redoubtable strength of tyranny's tentacles.

Never before has censorship been so perfect. Never before have those who are still led to believe, in a few countries, that they remain free citizens, been less entitled to make their opinions heard, wherever it is a matter of choices affecting their real lives. Never before has it been possible to lie to them so brazenly. The spectator is simply supposed to know nothing, and deserve nothing. Those who are always watching to see what happens next will never act: such must be the spectator's condition. People often cite the United States as an exception because there Nixon eventually came to grief with a series of denials whose clumsiness was too cynical: but this entirely local exception, for which there were some old historical causes, clearly no longer holds true, since Reagan has recently been able to do the same thing with impunity. Many things may be unauthorised; everything is permitted. Talk of scandal is thus archaic. The most profound summing-up of the period which the whole world entered shortly after Italy and the United States, can be found in the words of a senior Italian statesman, a member, simultaneously, of both the official government and the parallel government, P2, *Potere Due*: 'Once there were scandals, but not any more.'

In *The Eighteenth Brumaire of Louis Bonaparte*, Marx described the state's encroachment upon Second Empire France, then blessed with half a million bureaucrats: '[Everything was] made a subject for governmental activity, whether it was a bridge, a schoolhouse, the communal property of a village community, or the railways, the national wealth and the national university of France.' The famous question of the funding of political parties was already being posed, for Marx noted that, 'The parties that strove in turn for mastery regarded possession of this immense state edifice as the main booty for the victor.' Yet this may nonetheless sound somewhat bucolic and out of date, at a time when the state's speculations involve new towns and motorways, channel tunnels and nuclear energy, oil wells and computers, the administration of banks and cultural centres, the modification of the 'audiovisual landscape' and secret arms exports, property speculation and pharmaceuticals, agribusiness and hospitals, military credits and the secret funds of the ever-expanding departments charged with running society's numerous defence services. But Marx unfortunately remains all too up to date when in the same book he describes this government, which 'rather than deciding by night and striking by day, decides by day and strikes by night'.

IX

SUCH a perfect democracy constructs its own inconceivable foe, terrorism. Its wish is *to be judged by its enemies rather than by its results.* The story of terrorism is written by the state and it is therefore highly instructive. The spectators must certainly never know everything about terrorism, but they must always know enough to convince them that, compared with terrorism, everything else must be acceptable, or in any case more rational and democratic.

The modernisation of repression has succeeded in perfecting – first in the Italian pilot-project under the name of *pentiti* – sworn *professional accusers*; a phenomenon first seen in the seventeenth century after the Fronde, when such people were called 'certificated witnesses'. This spectacular judicial progress has filled Italy's prisons with thousands of people condemned to do penance for a civil war which did not take place, a kind of mass armed insurrection which, by chance, never actually happened, a putsch woven of such stuff as dreams are made on.

It can be seen that interpretations of terrorism's mysteries appear to have brought about a symmetry between contradictory views, rather like two schools of philosophy adhering to absolutely incompatible metaphysical systems. Some would see terrorism as simply a number of acts of blatant manipulation on the part of the secret services; others would reproach the terrorists for their total lack of historical understanding. But a little historical logic should rapidly convince us that there is nothing contradictory in recognising that people who understand nothing of history can readily be manipulated; even more so than others. And it is much easier to lead someone to 'repent' when it can be shown that everything he thought he did freely was actually known in advance. It is an inevitable consequence of clandestine, military forms of organisation that a few infiltrators can activate, and eliminate, a lot of people. Criticism, when evaluating armed struggles, must sometimes analyse particular operations without being led astray by the general resemblance that will finally be imposed on all of them. We should expect, as a logical possibility, that the state's security services intend to use all the advantages they find in the realm of the spectacle, which has indeed been organised with that in mind for some considerable time: on the contrary, it is a difficulty in perceiving this which is astonishing, and rings false.

Judicial repression's present objective here, of course, is to generalise matters as fast as possible. What is important in this commodity is the packing, or the labelling: the price codes. One enemy of spectacular democracy is the same as another, just like spectacular democracies themselves. Thus there must be no right of asylum for terrorists, and even those who have not yet been accused of being terrorists can certainly become them, with extradition swiftly following. In November 1978, dealing with the case of a young print worker, Gabor Winter, wanted by the West German government mainly for having printed certain revolutionary leaflets, Mlle Nicole Pradain, acting on behalf of the Department of Public Prosecution in the Appeal Court of Paris, quickly showed that the 'political motives' which could be the only grounds for refusing extradition under the Franco-German agreement of 29 November 1951, could not be invoked:

> Gabor Winter is a social criminal, not a political one. He refuses to accept social constraints. A true political criminal doesn't reject society. He attacks political structures and not, like Gabor Winter, social structures.

The notion of acceptable political crime only became recognised in Europe once the bourgeoisie had successfully attacked previous social structures. The nature of political crime could not be separated from the varied objectives of social critique. This was true for Blanqui, Varlin, Durruti. Nowadays there is a pretence of wishing to preserve a purely political crime, like some inexpensive luxury, a crime which doubtless no one will ever have the occasion to commit again, since no one is interested in the subject any more; except for the professional politicians themselves, whose crimes are rarely pursued, nor for that matter called political. All crimes and offences are effectively social. But of all social crimes, none must be seen as worse than the impertinent claim to still want to change something in a society which has so far been only too kind and patient; but *has had enough of being blamed.*

X

ACCORDING to the basic interests of the new system of domination, the dissolution of logic has been pursued by different, but mutually supportive, means. Some of these means involve the technology which the spectacle has tested and popularised; others are more linked to the mass psychology of submission.

At the technological level, when images chosen and constructed by *someone else* have everywhere become the individual's principal connection to the world he formerly observed for himself, it has certainly not been forgotten that these images can tolerate anything and everything; because within the same image all things can be juxtaposed without contradiction. The flow of images carries everything before it, and it is similarly someone else who controls at will this simplified summary of the sensible world; who decides where the flow will lead as well as the rhythm of what should be shown, like some perpetual, arbitrary surprise, leaving no time for reflection, and entirely independent of what the spectator might understand or think of it. In this concrete experience of permanent submission lies the psychological origin of such general acceptance of what is; an acceptance which comes to find in it, *ipso facto*, a sufficient value. Beyond what is strictly secret, spectacular discourse obviously silences anything it finds inconvenient. It isolates all it shows from its context, its past, its intentions and its consequences. It is thus completely illogical. Since no one may contradict it, it has the right to contradict itself, to correct its own past. The arrogant intention of its servants, when they have to put forward some new, and perhaps still more dishonest version of certain facts, is to harshly correct the ignorance and misinterpretations they attribute to their public, while the day before they themselves were busily disseminating the error, with their habitual assurance. Thus the spectacle's instruction and the spectators' ignorance are wrongly seen as antagonistic factors when in fact they give birth to each other. In the same way, the computer's binary language is an irresistible inducement to the continual and unreserved acceptance of what has been programmed according to the wishes of someone else and passes for the timeless source of a superior, impartial and total logic. Such progress, such speed, such breadth of vocabulary! Political? Social? Make your choice. You cannot have both. My own choice is inescapable. They are jeering at us, and we know whom these programs are for. Thus it is hardly surprising that children should enthusiastically start their education at an early age with the Absolute Knowledge of computer science; while they are still unable to read, for reading demands making judgements at every line; and is the only access to the wealth of pre-spectacular human experience. Conversation is almost dead, and soon so too will be those who knew how to speak.

The primary cause of the decadence of contemporary thought evidently lies in the fact that spectacular discourse leaves no room for any reply; while logic was only socially constructed through dialogue. Furthermore, when respect for those who speak through the spectacle is so widespread, when they are held to be rich, important, prestigious, to be *authority itself*, the spectators tend to want to be just as illogical as the spectacle, thereby proudly displaying an individual reflection of this authority. And finally, logic is not easy, and no one has tried to teach it. Drug addicts do not study logic; they no longer need it, nor are they capable of it. The spectator's laziness is shared by all intellectual functionaries and overnight specialists, all of whom do their best to conceal the narrow limits of their knowledge by the dogmatic repetition of arguments with illogical authority.

XI

IT IS generally believed that those who have displayed the greatest incapacity in matters of logic are self-proclaimed revolutionaries. This unjustified reproach dates from an age when almost everyone thought with some minimum of logic, with the striking exception of cretins and militants; and in the case of the latter bad faith played its part, intentionally, because it was held to be effective. But today there is no escaping the fact that intense absorption of the spectacle has, as we should have expected, turned most of our contemporaries into ideologues, if only in fits and starts, bits and pieces. Absence of logic, that is to say loss of the ability immediately to perceive what is significant and what is insignificant or irrelevant; what is incompatible or what could well be complementary; all that a particular consequence implies and at the same time all that it excludes – high doses of this disease have been intentionally injected into the population by the spectacle's *anaesthetists/resuscitators*. Rebels have certainly not been any more illogical than passive victims. It is simply that the former display a more intense manifestation of the generalised irrationality, because while parading their aims and programmes they have actually tried to carry out practical projects – even if it is only to read certain texts and show that they know what they mean. They have committed themselves to overcoming logic, even at the level of strategy, which is precisely the entire operational field of the dialectical logic of conflicts; but, like everyone else, they lack the basic ability to orient themselves by the old, imperfect tools of formal logic. No one worries about them; and hardly anyone thinks about the others.

The individual who has been more deeply marked by this impoverished spectacular thought than by *any other aspect of his experience* puts himself at the service of the established order right from the start, even though subjectively he may have had quite the opposite intention. He will essentially follow the language of the spectacle, for it is the only one he is familiar with; the one in which he learned to speak. No doubt he would like to be regarded as an enemy of its rhetoric; but he will use its syntax. This is one of the most important aspects of spectacular domination's success.

The swift disappearance of our former vocabulary is merely one moment in this process. It helps it along.

XII

THE erasure of the personality is the fatal accompaniment to an existence which is concretely submissive to the spectacle's rules, ever more removed from the possibility of authentic experience and thus from the discovery of individual preferences. Paradoxically, permanent self-denial is the price the individual pays for the tiniest bit of social status. Such an existence demands a fluid fidelity, a succession of continually disappointing commitments to false products. It is a matter of running hard to keep up with the inflation of devalued signs of life. Drugs help one to come to terms with this state of affairs, while madness allows one to escape from it.

In all sorts of business in this society, where the *distribution* of goods is centralised in such a way that it determines – both notoriously and secretly – the very definition of what could be desirable, it sometimes happens that certain people are attributed with knowledge, qualities, or even vices, all entirely imaginary, in order to explain the satisfactory development of particular enterprises. The only aim is to hide, or at least to disguise as far as possible, the working of various *agreements which decide everything.*

Yet despite its frequent intentions, and the redoubtable means at its disposal, to highlight the full stature of supposedly remarkable personalities,

present society more often only succeeds in demonstrating quite the opposite, and not merely in what has
today replaced the arts, or discussion of the arts. One
total incompetent will collide with another; panic
ensues and it is then simply a matter of who will fall
apart first. A lawyer, for example, forgetting that he is
supposed to represent one side in a trial, will be
genuinely swayed by the arguments of his opposite
number, even when these arguments are as hollow as
his own. It can also happen that an innocent suspect
temporarily confesses to a crime he did not commit
simply because he is impressed *by the logic* of an
informer who wants him to believe he is guilty (see
the case of Dr Archambeau in Poitiers, in 1984).

MacLuhan himself, the spectacle's first apologist,
who had seemed to be the most convinced imbecile of
the century, changed his mind when he finally
discovered in 1976 that 'the pressure of the mass
media leads to irrationality', and that it was becoming
urgent to modify their usage. The sage of Toronto had
formerly spent several decades marvelling at the
numerous freedoms created by a 'global village'
instantly and effortlessly accessible to all. Villages,
unlike towns, have always been ruled by conformism,
isolation, petty surveillance, boredom and repetitive
malicious gossip about the same families. Which is a
precise enough description of the global spectacle's
present vulgarity, in which it has become impossible

to distinguish the Grimaldi–Monaco or Bourbon–Franco dynasties from those who succeeded the Stuarts. However, MacLuhan's ungrateful modern disciples are now trying to make people forget him, hoping to establish their own careers in media celebration of all these new freedoms to 'choose' at random from ephemera. And no doubt they will retract their claims even faster than the man who inspired them.

XIII

THE spectacle makes no secret of the fact that certain dangers surround the wonderful order it has established. Ocean pollution and the destruction of equatorial forests threaten oxygen renewal; the earth's ozone layer is menaced by industrial growth; nuclear radiation accumulates irreversibly. It merely concludes that none of these things matter. It will only talk about dates and measures. And on these alone, it is successfully reassuring – something which a pre-spectacular mind would have thought impossible.

Spectacular democracy approaches matters with great subtlety, very different from the straightforward brutality of the totalitarian *diktat*. It can keep the original name for something secretly changed (beer, beef or philosophers). And it can just as easily change the name when the thing itself has been secretly maintained. In England, for example, the nuclear waste reprocessing plant at Windscale was renamed Sellafield in order to allay the suspicions which were aroused by a disastrous fire in 1957, though this toponymic reprocessing did nothing to limit the rise in local mortality rates from cancer and leukaemia. The British government, as the population democratically learned thirty years later, had decided to suppress a report on the catastrophe which it judged, reasonably enough, would probably shake public confidence in nuclear power.

The nuclear industry, both military and civil, demands a far higher dose of secrecy than in other fields – which already have plenty, as we know. To make life – that is to say, lying – easier for the sages chosen by the system's masters, it has been found useful also to change measurements, to vary them according to a large number of criteria, and refine them, so as to be able to juggle as necessary with a range of figures which are hard to convert. Hence, to measure radioactivity levels, one can choose from a range of units of measurement: curies, becquerels, roentgens, rads alias centigrays, and rems, not forgetting the humble millirads, and sieverts which are worth 100 rems. It reminds one of the old subdivisions of British currency which foreigners found so confusing, back in the days when Sellafield was still called Windscale.

One can imagine the rigour and precision which would have been achieved in the nineteenth century by military history, and thus by theorists of strategy, if, so as not to give too much confidential information to neutral commentators or enemy historians, campaigns were invariably described in the following manner:

> The preliminary phase involved a series of engagements in which, from our side, a strong advance force made up of four generals and the units under their command, met an enemy force of 13,000 bayonets. In the subsequent phase a fiercely disputed pitched battle developed, in which our entire army advanced, with 290 canons and a heavy cavalry of 18,000 sabres; the confronting enemy alignment comprised no less than 3,600 infantry lieutenants, 40 captains of hussars and 24 of cuirassiers. Following alternate advances and retreats on both sides, the battle can finally be seen as inconclusive. Our losses, somewhat lower than the average figure normally expected in combat of similar duration and intensity, were appreciably superior to those of the Greeks at Marathon, but remained inferior to those of the Prussians at Jena.

In this example, it is not impossible for a specialist to gather some vague idea of the forces engaged. But the conduct of operations remains securely concealed.

In June 1987, Pierre Bacher, deputy director of installations at Electricité de France, revealed the latest safety doctrine for nuclear power stations. By installing valves and filters it becomes much easier to avoid major catastrophes, like cracks or explosions in the reactors, which would affect a whole 'region'. Such catastrophes are produced by excessive containment. Whenever the plant looks like blowing, it is better to decompress gently, showering only a restricted area of a few kilometres, an area which on each occasion will be differently and haphazardly extended depending on the wind. He discloses that in the past two years discreet experiments carried out at Cadarache, in the Drôme, 'clearly showed that waste – essentially gas – is infinitesimal, representing at worst one per cent of the radioactivity in the power station itself.' Thus a very moderate worst case: one per cent. Formerly, we were assured there was no risk at all, except in the case of accidents, which were logically impossible. The experience of the first few years changed this reasoning as follows: since accidents can always happen, what must be avoided is their reaching a catastrophic threshold, and that is easy. All that is necessary is to contaminate little by little, in moderation. Who would not agree that it is infinitely healthier to limit yourself to an intake of 140 centilitres of vodka per day for several years, rather than getting drunk right away like the Poles?

It is indeed unfortunate that human society should encounter such burning problems just when it has become materially impossible to make heard the least objection to the language of the commodity; just when power – quite rightly because it is shielded by the spectacle from any response to its piecemeal and delirious decisions and justifications – *believes that it no longer needs to think*; and indeed can no longer think. Would not even the staunchest democrat have preferred to have been given more intelligent masters?

At the international conference of experts held in Geneva in December 1986 the question was quite simply whether to introduce a worldwide ban on the production of chlorofluorocarbons (CFCs), the gases which have recently and rapidly started to destroy the thin layer of ozone which – as will be recalled – protects this planet against the harmful effects of solar rays. Daniel Verilhe, representing Elf-Aquitaine's chemicals subsidiary, and in this capacity part of a French delegation firmly opposed to any ban, made a sensible point: 'It will take at least three years to develop substitutes and the costs will be quadrupled.' As we know, this fugitive ozone layer, so high up, belongs to no one and has no market value. This *industrial* strategist could thus show his opponents the extent of their inexplicable disregard for economics: 'It is highly dangerous to base an industrial strategy on environmental imperatives.'

Those who long ago had embarked on a critique of
political economy by defining it as 'the final denial of
humanity' were not mistaken. This will be seen as its
defining characteristic.

XIV

IT IS sometimes said that science today is subservient
to the imperatives of profit, but that is nothing new.
What is new is the way the economy has now come to
declare open war on humanity, attacking not only our
possibilities for living, but our chances of survival. It is
here that science – renouncing the opposition to
slavery that formed a significant part of its own
history – has chosen to put itself at the service of spectacular domination. Until it got to this point, science
possessed a relative autonomy. It knew how to understand its own portion of reality; and in this has made
an immense contribution to increasing economic
resources. When an all-powerful economy lost its
reason – *and that is precisely what defines these spectacular
times* – it suppressed the last vestiges of scientific autonomy, both in methodology and, by the same token,
in the practical working conditions of its 'researchers'.
No longer is science asked to understand the world,
or to improve any part of it. It is asked instead to

immediately justify everything that happens. As stupid in this field, which it exploits with the most ruinous disregard, as it is everywhere else, spectacular domination has cut down the vast tree of scientific knowledge in order to make itself a truncheon. To obey this ultimate social demand for a manifestly impossible justification, it is better not to be able to think at all, but rather to be well trained in the conveniences of spectacular language. And it is in such a career that the prostituted science of our despicable times has found its latest specialisation, with goodwill and alacrity.

The science of lying justifications naturally appeared with the first symptoms of bourgeois society's decadence, with the cancerous proliferation of those pseudo-sciences known as 'human'; yet modern medicine, for example, had once been able to pass as useful, and those who eradicated smallpox or leprosy were very different from those who contemptibly capitulated in the face of nuclear radiation or chemical farming. It can readily be seen, of course, that medicine today no longer has the right to defend public health against a pathogenic environment, for that would be to challenge the state, or at least the pharmaceuticals industry. But it is not only by its obligation to keep quiet that contemporary science acknowledges what it has become. It is also by its frequent and artless outbursts. In November 1985, professors Even and Andrieu at Laënnec hospital announced that they had perhaps found an effective cure for Aids, following an experiment on four patients which had lasted a week. Two days later, the patients having died, several other doctors, whose research was not so far advanced, or who were perhaps jealous, expressed certain reservations as to the professors' precipitate haste in broadcasting what was merely the misleading appearance of victory – a few hours before the patients' condition finally deteriorated. Even and Andrieu defended themselves nonchalantly, arguing that 'after all, false hopes are better than no hope at all.' Their ignorance was too great for them to recognise this argument as a precise and complete disavowal of the spirit of science; as the one which had historically always served to endorse the profitable daydreams of charlatans and sorcerers, long before such people were put in charge of hospitals.

When official science has come to such a pass, like all the rest of the social spectacle that for all its materially modernised and enhanced presentation is merely reviving the ancient techniques of fairground mountebanks – *illusionists, barkers and stool-pigeons* – it is not surprising to see a similar and widespread revival of the authority of seers and sects, of vacuum-packed Zen or Mormon theology. Ignorance, which has always served the authorities well, has also always been exploited by ingenious ventures on the fringes of the law. And what better moment than one where illiteracy has become so widespread? But this reality in its turn is denied by a new display of sorcery. From its inception, Unesco had adopted a very precise scientific definition of the illiteracy which it strove to combat in backward countries. When the same phenomenon was unexpectedly seen to be returning, but this time in the so-called advanced nations, rather in the way that the one who was waiting for Grouchy instead saw Blücher join the battle, it was simply a matter of calling in the Guard of experts; they carried the day with a single, unstoppable assault, replacing *the word* illiteracy by 'language difficulties': just as a 'false patriot' can sometimes arrive at an opportune moment to support a good national cause. And to ensure that the pertinence of this neologism was, between pedagogues, carved in stone, a new definition was quickly handed round, as if it had always been accepted – according to which, while the illiterate was, as we know, someone who had never learnt to read, those with language difficulties in the modern sense are on the contrary people who had learnt to read (and had even learnt *better* than before, coolly proposed the more gifted official theorists and historians of pedagogy), but who had by chance immediately *forgotten again*. This surprising explanation might have been more disturbing than reassuring, if, by deliberately missing the point, it had not skilfully sidestepped the first consequence which would have come to anyone's mind in more scientific eras. That is, the recognition that this new phenomenon had itself to be explained and combatted, since it had never been observed or even imagined anywhere before the recent progress of damaged thought, when analytical and practical decadence go hand in hand.

XV

MORE than a century ago, A.-L. Sardou's *Nouveau Dictionnaire des Synonymes français* defined the nuances which must be grasped between: *fallacious, deceptive, impostrous, inveigling, insidious, captious*; and which taken together constitute today a kind of palette of colours with which to paint a portrait of the society of the spectacle. It was beyond the scope of his time, and his specialist experience, to distinguish with equal clarity the related, but very different, meanings of the perils normally expected to be faced by any group which practises subversion, following, for example, this progression: *misguided, provoked, infiltrated, manipulated, taken over, subverted.* Certainly these important nuances have never been appreciated by the doctrinaires of 'armed struggle'.

Fallacious [*fallacieux*], from the Latin *fallaciosus*, adept at or accustomed to deception, full of deceit: the definition of this adjective is equivalent to the superlative of *deceptive* [*trompeur*]. That which deceives or leads into error in any way is *deceptive*: that which is done in order to deceive, abuse, lead into error by plan intended to deceive with artifice and misleading device most calculated to abuse, is *fallacious*. *Deceptive* is a generic and vague word; all forms of uncertain signs and appearance, are *deceptive*: *fallacious* denotes duplicity, deceit, studied imposture; sophistic speech, asseveration or reasoning is *fallacious*. The word has affinities with *impostrous* [*imposteur*], *inveigling* [*séducteur*], *insidious* [*insidieux*] and *captious* [*captieux*], but without equivalence. *Impostrous* denotes all forms of false appearance, or conspiracies to abuse or injure; for example, hypocrisy, calumny, etc. *Inveigling* expresses action calculated to take possession of someone, to lead them astray by artful and insinuating means. *Insidious* only indicates the act of placing traps and entrapping. *Captious* is restricted to the subtle act of taking by surprise and taking in. *Fallacious* encompasses most of these definitions.

XVI

THE relatively new concept of *disinformation* was recently imported from Russia, along with a number of other inventions useful in the running of modern states. It is openly employed by particular powers, or, consequently, by people who hold fragments of economic or political authority, in order to maintain what is established; and always in a *counter-offensive* role. Whatever can oppose a single official truth must necessarily be disinformation emanating from hostile or at least rival powers, and would have been intentionally and malevolently falsified. Disinformation would not be simple negation of a fact which suits the authorities, or the simple affirmation of a fact which does not suit them: that is called psychosis. Unlike the straightforward lie, disinformation must inevitably contain a degree of truth but one deliberately manipulated by an artful enemy. That is what makes it so attractive to the defenders of the dominant society. The power which speaks of disinformation does not believe itself to be absolutely faultless, but knows that it can attribute to any precise criticism the excessive insignificance which characterises disinformation; with the result that it will never have to admit to any particular fault.

In essence, disinformation would be a travesty of the truth. Whoever disseminates it is culpable, whoever believes it is stupid. But who precisely would this artful enemy be? In this case, it cannot be terrorism, which is in no danger of 'disinforming' anyone, since it is charged with ontologically representing the grossest and least acceptable *error*. Thanks to its etymology and to present memories of those limited confrontations which around mid-century briefly opposed East and West, concentrated spectacle and diffuse spectacle, the capitalism of today's integrated spectacle still pretends to believe that the capitalism of bureaucratic totalitarianism – sometimes even presented as the terrorists' base camp or inspiration – remains its fundamental enemy, despite the innumerable proofs of their profound alliance and solidarity. But actually all established powers, despite certain genuine local rivalries, and without ever wanting to spell it out, never forget what one of the rare German internationalists after the outbreak of the First World War managed to recall (on the side of subversion and without any great immediate success): 'The main enemy is within.' In the end, disinformation is the equivalent of what was represented in the nineteenth-century language of social war as 'dangerous passions'. It is all that is obscure and threatens to oppose the unprecedented happiness which we know this society offers to those who trust it, a happiness which greatly outweighs various insignificant risks and disappointments. And everyone who *sees* this happiness in the spectacle agrees that we should not grumble about its price; everyone else is a disinformer.

The other advantage derived from denouncing a particular instance of disinformation in this way is that it wards off any suspicion that the spectacle's global language might contain the same thing. With the most scientific assurance, the spectacle can identify the only place where disinformation could be found: in anything which can be said that might displease it.

It is doubtless by mistake – unless it be a deliberate decoy – that a project was recently set in motion in France to place a kind of official label on some parts of the media guaranteeing them 'free from disinformation'. This wounded certain media professionals, who still believe, or more modestly would still like it to be believed, that until now they had not actually been subject to censorship. But the concept of disinformation must never be used *defensively*, still less as part of a static defence, building a Great Wall or Maginot Line around an area supposedly out of bounds to disinformation. There must be disinformation, and it must be something fluid and potentially ubiquitous. Where the language of the spectacle is not under attack it would be foolish to defend it; and the concept would wear out very fast indeed if one were to try to defend it against all the evidence on points which ought on the contrary to be kept from public view. Moreover the authorities have no real need to guarantee that any particular information does not contain disinformation. Nor have they the means to do so: they are not respected to that extent, and would only draw down suspicion on the information concerned. The concept of disinformation is only valid for counter-attack. It must be kept in reserve, then rapidly thrown into the fray to drive back any truth which has managed to get through.

If occasionally a kind of unregulated disinformation threatens to appear, in the service of particular interests temporarily in conflict, and threatens to be believed, getting out of control and thus clashing with the concerted work of a less irresponsible disinformation, there is no reason to fear that the former involves other manipulators who are more subtle or more skilled: it is simply because disinformation now spreads *in a world where there is no room for verification.*

The confusionist concept of disinformation is pushed into the limelight immediately to refute, by its very name, any criticism that has failed to eliminate the diverse agencies of the organisation of silence. For example it could one day be said, should this seem desirable, that this text was an attempt to disinform about the spectacle; or indeed, since it is the same thing, that it was a piece of disinformation harmful to democracy.

Contrary to its spectacular definition, the practice of disinformation can only serve the state here and now, under its direct command, or at the initiative of those who uphold the same values. Disinformation is actually inherent in all existing information; and indeed is its main characteristic. It is only named where passivity must be maintained by intimidation. Where disinformation is *named*, it does not exist. Where it exists, it is not named.

When there were still conflicting ideologies, which claimed to be for or against some recognised aspect of reality, there were fanatics, and liars, but there were no 'disinformers'. When respect for the spectacular consensus, or at least a desire for spectacular kudos, prohibits any honest declaration of what someone is against, or equally what he wholeheartedly approves; and when at the same time he needs to disguise a part of what he is supposed to acknowledge because for one reason or another it is considered dangerous, then he employs disinformation; as if by blunder or negligence, or by *pretended* false reasoning. In political activity after 1968, for example, the incompetent recuperators known as 'pro-situs', became *the first disinformers* because they did their best to hide all practical manifestations which confirmed the critique they claimed to have adopted; and, without the slightest embarrassment at weakening its expression, never referred to anything or anyone, in order to suggest that they themselves had actually discovered something.

XVII

REVERSING Hegel's famous maxim, I noted as long ago as 1967 that 'in a world that has *really* been turned upside down, truth is a moment of falsehood'. In the intervening years, this principle has encroached upon each specific domain, without exception.

Thus in an era when contemporary art can no longer exist, it becomes difficult to judge classical art. Here as elsewhere, ignorance is only created in order to be exploited. As the meanings of history and taste are lost, networks of falsification are organised. It is only necessary to control the experts and auctioneers, which is easy enough, to arrange everything, since in this kind of business – and at the end of the day in every other kind – it is the sale which authenticates the value. Afterwards it is the collectors and museums, particularly in America, who, gorged on falsehood, will have an interest in upholding its good reputation, just as the International Monetary Fund maintains the fiction of a positive value in the huge debts of dozens of countries.

What is false creates taste, and reinforces itself by knowingly eliminating any possible reference to the authentic. And what is genuine is *reconstructed* as quickly as possible, to resemble the false. Being the richest and the most modern, the Americans have been the main dupes of this traffic in false art. And they are exactly the same people who pay for restoration work at Versailles or in the Sistine Chapel. This is why Michelangelo's frescoes will acquire the fresh, bright colours of a cartoon strip, and the genuine furniture at Versailles, the sparkling gilt which will make them resemble the fake Louis XIV suites imported by Texans at such great expense.

Feuerbach's judgement on the fact that his time preferred 'the sign to the thing signified, the copy to the original, fancy to reality', has been thoroughly vindicated by the century of the spectacle, and in several spheres where the nineteenth century preferred to keep its distance from what was already its fundamental nature: industrial capitalism. Thus it was that the bourgeoisie had widely disseminated the rigorous mentality of the museum, the original object, precise historical criticism, the authentic document. Today, however, the tendency to replace the real with the artificial is ubiquitous. In this regard, it is fortuitous that traffic pollution has necessitated the replacement of the Marly Horses in place de la Concorde, or the Roman statues in the doorway of Saint-Trophime in Arles, by plastic replicas. Everything will be more beautiful than before, for the tourists' cameras.

The high point in this process has doubtless been reached by the Chinese bureaucracy's laughable fake of the vast terracotta *industrial army* of the First Emperor, which so many visiting statesmen have been taken to admire *in situ*. A clear demonstration, since it was possible to fool them so cruelly, that in all their hordes of advisors, there is not one single individual who knows about art history in China, or anywhere else – 'Your Excellency's computers have no data on this subject.' Such a confirmation of the fact that for the first time in history it is possible to govern without the slightest understanding of art or of what is authentic and what is impossible, could alone suffice to make us suppose that the credulous fools who run the economy and the administration will probably lead the world to some great catastrophe; if their actual practice had not already made that crystal clear.

XVIII

OUR society is built on secrecy, from the 'front' organisations which draw an impenetrable screen over the concentrated wealth of their members, to the 'official secrets' which allow the state a vast field of operation free from any legal constraint; from the often frightening secrets of *shoddy production* hidden by advertising, to the projections of an extrapolated future, in which domination alone reads off the likely progress of things whose existence it denies, calculating the responses it will mysteriously make. Some observations can be made on these matters.

There are ever more places in cities and in the countryside which remain inaccessible, that is to say protected and shielded from public gaze; which are out of bounds to the innocently curious, and well guarded against espionage. Without all being strictly military, they follow the military model in preventing any prying incursion by local people or passers-by; or even by the police, whose functions have long been reduced to mere surveillance and repression of the most commonplace forms of delinquency. Thus it was that when Aldo Moro was a prisoner of *Potere Due* he was held, not in a building which could not be found, but in one which could not be entered.

There are ever more people trained to act in secret, prepared and practised for that alone. There are special units armed with confidential archives, that is to say with secret data and analysis. There are others armed with a range of techniques for the exploitation and manipulation of these secrets. And finally there are the 'active' units, equipped with other means to simplify the problems in question.

The resources allocated to these specialists in surveillance and influence continue to increase, while general circumstances favour them more by the year. When, for example, the new conditions of integrated spectacular society have driven its critique into genuine clandestinity, not because it is in hiding but *because it is hidden* by the ponderous stage-management of diversionary thought, those who are nonetheless responsible for its surveillance, and in the end for its denial, can now employ traditional methods for operations in clandestine milieux: provocation, infiltration, and various forms of elimination of authentic critique in favour of a false one which will have been created for this purpose. When the spectacle's general imposture is enriched with recourse to a thousand individual impostures, uncertainty grows at every turn. An unexplained crime can also be called suicide, in prison as elsewhere; the collapse of logic allows trials and inquiries which soar into irrationality, and which are frequently falsified right from the start through absurd autopsies, performed by extraordinary experts.

We have long been accustomed to summary executions of all kinds of people. Known terrorists, or those considered as such, are openly fought with terrorist methods. Mossad can arrange the killing of Abou Jihad, the SAS can do the same with Irish people, and the parallel police of GAL with Basques. Those whose killings are arranged by supposed terrorists are not chosen without reason; but it is generally impossible to be sure of understanding these reasons. One can be aware that Bologna railway station was blown up to ensure that Italy continued to be well governed; or of the identity of the 'death squads' in

Brazil; or that the Mafia can burn down a hotel in the United States to facilitate a racket. But how can we know what purpose was ultimately served by the 'mad killers of Brabant'? It is hard to apply the principle *Cui prodest?* where so many active interests are so well concealed. The result is that under the rule of the integrated spectacle, we live and die at the confluence of innumerable mysteries.

Media/police rumours acquire instantly – or at worst after three or four repetitions – the indisputable status of age-old historical evidence. By the legendary authority of the spectacle of the day, odd characters eliminated in silence can reappear as fictive survivors, whose return can always be conjured up or computed, and *proved* by the mere say-so of specialists. They exist somewhere between the Acheron and the Lethe, these dead whom the spectacle has not properly buried, supposedly slumbering while awaiting the summons which will awake them all: home is the pirate, home from the sea, and the terrorist home from the hill; home, too, the thief who no longer needs to steal.

Thus is uncertainty organised everywhere. Often domination will protect itself by *false attacks*, whose media coverage covers up the true operation. Such was the case with the bizarre assault on the Spanish Cortes by Tejero and his civil guards in 1981, whose failure had to hide another more modern, that is to say more disguised *pronunciamiento*, which succeeded.

The equally showy failure of the French secret services' sabotage attempt in New Zealand in 1985 has sometimes been seen as a stratagem, perhaps designed to divert attention from the numerous new uses of these secret services, by persuading people of their caricatural clumsiness both in their choice of target and in their mode of operation. It has most certainly been almost universally accepted that the geological explorations for oil-beds in the subsoil of *the city of Paris*, so noisily conducted in the autumn of 1986, had no other serious purpose than to measure the inhabitants' current level of stupefaction and submission; by showing them supposed research so absolutely devoid of economic reason.

So mysterious has power become that after the affair of the illegal arms sales to Iran by the US presidency, one might wonder who was really running the United States, the leading power in the so-called democratic world. And thus who the hell was running the democratic world?

More profoundly, in this world which is officially so respectful of economic necessities, no one ever knows the real cost of anything which is produced. In fact the major part of the real cost *is never calculated; and the rest is kept secret.*

XIX

AT the beginning of 1988, a certain General Noriega suddenly became world famous. He was the unofficial dictator of Panama, a country without an army, where he commanded the National Guard. Panama is not really a sovereign state: it was dug out for its canal, rather than the reverse. Its currency is the dollar, and the army which runs it is similarly foreign. Noriega had thus devoted his entire career – precisely like Jaruzelski in Poland – to serving the occupying power as its chief of police. He imported drugs into the United States, since Panama was not bringing him sufficient revenue, and exported his 'Panamanian' capital to Switzerland. He had worked with the CIA against Cuba and, to provide adequate cover for his business activities, had also denounced some of his rivals in the import trade to the US authorities, obsessed as they are with this problem. To the envy of Washington, his chief security advisor was the best on the market: Michael Harari, a former officer with Mossad, the Israeli secret service. When the Americans finally decided to get rid of this character, some of their courts having carelessly condemned him, Noriega proclaimed that he was ready to defend himself for a thousand years – against foreigners, and against his own rebellious people; in the name of anti-imperialism he quickly received public support from

the more austere bureaucratic dictators in Cuba and
Nicaragua.

Far from being a peculiarly Panamanian phenomenon, this General Noriega, who *sells everything and
fakes everything*, in a world which does precisely the
same thing, was altogether a perfect representative of
the integrated spectacle, and of the successes it allows
the assorted managers of its internal and external politics: a sort of statesman in a sort of state, a sort of
general, a capitalist. He is the very model of *our modern
prince*, and of those destined to come to power and
stay there, the most able resemble him closely. It is not
Panama which produces such marvels, it is our times.

XX

FOR any intelligence service, following Clausewitz's
accurate theory of war, *knowledge* must become *power*.
From this these services derive their contemporary
prestige, their peculiarly poetic quality. Whilst intelligence itself has been so throughly expelled from the
spectacle, which prohibits action and says very little
about the actions of others, it seems to have taken
refuge with those who analyse certain realities, and act
secretly on certain realities. The recent revelations
that Margaret Thatcher tried in vain to suppress, and

in fact confirmed by the attempt, have shown that in Britain these services have already been capable of bringing down a prime minister whose politics they deemed dangerous. The general contempt created by the spectacle thus, for new reasons, restored the fascination of what in Kipling's day was called 'the great game'.

'The conspiracy theory of history' was in the nineteenth century a reactionary and ridiculous belief, at a time when so many powerful social movements were stirring up the masses. Today's pseudo-rebels are well aware of this, thanks to hearsay or a few books, and believe that it remains true for eternity. They refuse to recognise the real praxis of their time; it is too sad for their cold hopes. The state notes this fact, and plays on it.

When almost every aspect of international political life and ever more important aspects of internal politics are conducted and displayed in the style of the secret services, with decoys, disinformation and double explanations (one *may* conceal another, or may only seem to) the spectacle confines itself to revealing a wearisome world of necessary incomprehensibility. This tedious series of lifeless, inconclusive crime novels has all the dramatic interest of a realistically staged fight between blacks, at night, in a tunnel.

When television has shown a fine picture and explained it with a brazen lie, idiots believe that everything is clear. The demi-elite is content to know that almost everything is obscure, ambivalent, 'constructed' by unknown codes. A more exclusive elite would like to know what is true, hard as it is to distinguish in each particular case despite all their access to special knowledge and confidences. Which is why they would like to get to know the method of truth, though their love usually remains unrequited.

XXI

SECRECY dominates this world, and first and foremost as the secret of domination. According to the spectacle, secrecy would only be a necessary exception to the rule of freely available, abundant information, just as domination in the integrated spectacle's 'free world' would be restricted to a mere executive body in the service of democracy. But no one really believes the spectacle. How then do spectators accept the existence of secrecy which alone rules out any chance of their running a world whose principal realities they know nothing, in the unlikely event that they were to be asked how to set about it? The fact is that almost no one sees secrecy in its inaccessible purity and its functional universality. Everyone accepts that there are inevitably little areas of secrecy reserved for specialists; as regards things in general, many believe they are *in on the secret.*

In his *Discours sur la servitude volontaire,* La Boétie showed how a tyrant's power will be considerably reinforced by the concentric circles of individuals who believe, rightly or wrongly, that it is in their interests to support it. In the same way many politicians and media professionals who are flattered not to be suspected of being *irresponsible,* learn a lot through their connections and confidences. Someone who is happy to be given confidential information is hardly likely to criticise it; nor to notice that in all that is confided to him, the principal part of reality is invariably hidden. Thanks to the benevolent protection of his deceivers, he sees a few more of the cards, false though they may be; he never learns the rules of the game. Thus he immediately identifies with the manipulators and scorns an ignorance which in fact he shares. For the titbits of information tossed to the familiars of a lying tyranny are usually poisoned with lies, manipulated and uncheckable. Yet they gratify those who get them, for they feel themselves superior to those who know nothing. Their only role is to make domination more respectable, never to make it comprehensible. They are the privilege of *front-row spectators* who are stupid enough to believe they can understand something, not by making use of what is hidden from them, but *by believing what is revealed*!

Domination has at least sufficient lucidity to expect that its free and unhindered reign will very shortly lead to a significant number of major catastrophes, both ecological (chemical, for example) and economic (in banking, for example). It has for some time been ensuring it is in a position to deal with these exceptional misfortunes by other means than its usual gentle use of disinformation.

XXII

AS TO the rising number of assassinations over the last two decades (Kennedy, Aldo Moro, Olaf Palme, ministers and bankers, a pope or two, some others who were worth more than all of them) which have remained completely unsolved – for while the odd supernumerary has been sacrificed there has never been any question of apprehending those who hold the purse strings – their serial character shows a common hallmark: the blatant, and variable, lies of official statements. The syndrome of this newly established social disease has quickly spread, as if, following the first documented cases, it *moved down* from the summits of the state (the traditional sphere for such crimes) and at the same time *moved up* from the lower depths, the other traditional locale for trafficking and protection rackets, where this kind of war has always gone on, between professionals. These activities tend to meet up in the *middle* of social affairs, a place which the state was prepared to frequent and which the Mafia was pleased to reach; thus a kind of confluence begins.

There has been no shortage of attempts to explain these new mysteries in terms of accidents: police incompetence, stupid magistrates, untimely press revelations, crisis of growth in the secret services, malevolent witnesses, or police spies suddenly deciding to go on strike. But Edgar Allan Poe had already discovered the real path to truth, in a well-known argument in 'The Murders in the Rue Morgue':

> It appears to me that this mystery is considered insoluble, for the very reason which should cause it to be regarded as easy of solution – I mean for the *outré* character of its features.... In investigations such as we are now pursuing, it should not be so much asked 'what has occurred', as 'what has occurred that has never occurred before'.

XXIII

IN January 1988 the Colombian drug Mafia issued a communiqué aimed at correcting public opinion about its supposed existence. Now the first requirement of any Mafia, wherever it may be, is naturally to prove that it does not exist, or that it has been the victim of unscientific calumnies; and that is the first thing it has in common with capitalism. But in these particular circumstances, this Mafia was so irritated at being the only one placed under the spotlight that it went so far as to give details of the other groupings who were trying to cover themselves by illegitimately using it as a scapegoat. It declared: 'We ourselves don't belong to the Mafia of politicians and bureaucrats, bankers, financiers or millionaires, nor to the Mafia of fraudulent contracts, monopolies or oil, nor to the media Mafia.'

We can doubtless assume that the authors of this statement have, like all the rest, an interest in diverting their own activities into that vast river of troubled water whose course irrigates the whole of present society, a river of crime and more banal illegalities. But it is also correct to assume that here we have people who by their very profession know better than most what they are talking about. The Mafia flourishes in the soil of contemporary society. Its expansion is as rapid as that of all the other products of the labour by which integrated spectacular society shapes its world. The Mafia grows along with the swift development of information technology and industrial food processing, along with urban redevelopment and shanty-towns, secret services and illiteracy.

XXIV

WHEN it was first brought to the United States by migrant Sicilian workers, the Mafia was nothing but an uprooted archaism; just like the gang wars between Chinese secret societies which appeared at the same time on the West Coast. Born out of obscurantism and poverty, the Mafia at that time was not even able to put down roots in Northern Italy. It seemed condemned to vanish with the progress of the modern state. For it was a form of organised crime which could only prosper through the 'protection' of backward minorities, outside the urban world, where the laws of the bourgeoisie and a rational police force could not penetrate. In its defence, the Mafia could only eliminate witnesses, to neutralise the police and judiciary, and to maintain necessary secrecy in its sphere of activity. But subsequently it found fresh scope in the *new obscurantism* first of diffuse spectacular society, then of its integrated form: with the total victory of secrecy, the general resignation of the populace, the complete loss of logic, the universal progress of venality and cowardice, all the conditions were in place for it to become a modern, and offensive, power.

Prohibition in America (one of the finest examples this century of the state's pretension to be able to exercise authoritarian control over everything, and of the results which ensue) handed over the trade in alcohol to organised crime for more than a decade. From there the Mafia, with its new wealth and experience, moved into electoral politics, commerce, the development of the market in professional killers, and certain aspects of international politics. During the Second World War it received favours from the US government, to help with the invasion of Sicily. Legalised alcohol was replaced by drugs, now the leading commodity in illegal consumption. Next the Mafia became closely involved in property dealing, in banking and in high-level politics and affairs of state, and then in the spectacular industries: television, films and publishing. And already, in the United States at least, it is involved in the music industry, as in every other activity where promotion depends on a relatively concentrated group of people. It is easy to apply pressure to them, with bribes and intimidation, since there is no shortage of capital or of untouchable, anonymous hitmen. By corrupting the disc-jockeys one can choose what will succeed, from equally wretched commodities.

But it is undoubtedly in Italy that the Mafia has acquired the greatest strength, in the wake of its experience and conquests in America. Since the period of its historic compromise with the parallel government it has been able to kill magistrates and police chiefs with impunity – a practice it inaugurated through its participation in the displays of political 'terrorism'. The similar evolution of the Mafia's Japanese equivalent, in relatively independent conditions, well illustrates the unity of the epoch.

It is always a mistake to try to explain something by opposing Mafia and state: they are never rivals. Theory easily verifies what all the rumours in practical life have all too easily shown. The Mafia is not an outsider in this world; it is perfectly at home. Indeed, in the integrated spectacle it stands as the *model* of all advanced commercial enterprises.

XXV

WITH the new conditions which now predominate in a society crushed under the spectacle's *iron heel*, we know, for example, that a political assassination can be presented in another light, can in a sense be screened. Everywhere the mad are more numerous than before, but what is infinitely more useful is that they can be talked about *madly*. And it is not some kind of reign of terror which forces such explanations on the media. On the contrary, it is the peaceful existence of such explanations which should cause terror.

When in 1914 with war on the horizon Villain assassinated Jaurès, no one doubted that Villain, though certainly a somewhat unbalanced man, had believed he had to kill Jaurès because in the eyes of the extremists of the patriotic right who had deeply influenced him, Jaurès seemed certain to have a detrimental effect on the country's defence. These extremists had merely underestimated the tremendous strength of patriotic commitment within the Socialist Party, which would immediately lead them into the *union sacrée*, whether or not Jaurès was assassinated or allowed to hold to his internationalist position in rejecting war. If such an event happened today, journalists/police and pundits on 'social issues' and 'terrorism', would quickly explain that Villain was well known for having planned several attempted murders, whose intended victims were always men who, despite the variety of their political opinions, all by chance looked and dressed rather like Jaurès. Psychiatrists would confirm this, and the *media*, merely confirming in their turn what the psychiatrists had said, would thus confirm their own competence and impartiality as *uniquely* authoritative experts. The official police investigation would immediately come up with several reputable people ready to bear witness to the fact that this same Villain, considering he had been rudely served at the 'Chope du Croissant', had in their presence loudly threatened to take revenge on its proprietor by publicly murdering on the premises one of his best customers.

This is not to say that in the past truth was revealed

often or quickly; for Villain was eventually acquitted by the French courts. He was not shot until 1936, at the start of the Spanish revolution, having been imprudent enough to move to the Balearic Islands.

XXVI

THE ubiquitous growth of secret societies and networks of influence answers the imperative demand of the new conditions for profitable management of economic affairs, at a time when the state holds a hegemonic role in the direction of production and when demand for all commodities depends strictly on the centralisation achieved by spectacular information/promotion, to which forms of distribution must also adapt. It is therefore only a natural product of the concentration of capital, production and distribution. Whatever does not grow must disappear; and no business can grow without adopting the values, techniques and methods of today's industry, spectacle and state. In the final analysis it is the particular form of development chosen by the economy of our epoch which dictates *the widespread creation of new personal bonds of dependency and protection.*

It is precisely here that we can see the profound truth of the Sicilian Mafia's maxim, so well appreciated throughout Italy: 'When you've got money and friends, you can laugh at the law.' In the integrated spectacle, *the laws are asleep*; because they were not made for the new production techniques, and because they are evaded in distribution by new types of agreement. What the public thinks, or prefers, is of no importance. This is what is hidden by the spectacle of all these opinion polls, elections, modernising restructurings. No matter who the winners are, the faithful customers *will get the worst of it*, because that is exactly what has been produced for them.

The widespread talk of a 'legal state' only dates from the moment when the modern, so-called democratic state generally ceased to be one. The fact that the expression was only popularised shortly after 1970 and, appropriately, in Italy is far from accidental. In many fields, laws are even made precisely *so that they may be evaded*, by those who have the means to do so. Illegality in some circumstances – for example, around the world trade in all sorts of weaponry, especially the most technologically sophisticated products – is simply a kind of back-up for the economic operation, which will be all the more profitable because of it. Today many business deals are necessarily *as dishonest as the century*, and not like those once made within a strictly limited range by people who had chosen the paths of dishonesty.

With the growth of promotion/control networks

to mark out and maintain exploitable sectors of the market, there is also an increase in the number of personal services which must be provided to those in the know, who have willingly provided their help; and these are not always the police or guardians of the state's interests and security. Functional complicities operate across time and distance, for their networks command all the means to impose those sentiments of gratitude and fidelity which were unfortunately so rare in the free activity of the bourgeois epoch.

One always learns something from one's adversary. We should not doubt that statesmen, too, came to read the young Lukàcs' remarks on the concepts of legality and illegality, at the time when they had to deal with the brief passage of a new generation of negativity – as Homer said, 'Men in their generations are like the leaves of the trees.' Since then statesmen, like us, have ceased to trouble themselves with any kind of ideology on the question; and indeed the practices of spectacular society no longer encourage ideological illusions of this kind. And finally it could be said of all of us that what has stopped us from devoting ourselves to one particular illegal activity is the fact that we have had several.

XXVII

IN book VIII, chapter 5 of *The Peloponnesian War*, Thucydides wrote something about the operations of another oligarchic conspiracy which closely relates to the situation in which we find ourselves:

> Nevertheless the Assembly and the Council chosen by lot still continued to hold meetings. However, they took no decisions that were not approved by the party of the revolution; in fact all the speakers were from this party, and what they were going to say had been considered by the party beforehand. People were afraid when they saw their numbers, and no one now dared to speak in opposition to them. If anyone did venture to do so, some appropriate method was soon found for having him killed, and no one tried to investigate such crimes or take action against those suspected of them. Instead the people kept quiet, and were in such a state of terror that they thought themselves lucky enough to be left unmolested even if they had said nothing at all. They imagined that the revolutionary party was much bigger than it really was, and they lost all confidence in themselves, being unable to find out the facts because of the size of the city and because they had insufficient knowledge of each other. For the same reason it was impossible for anyone who felt himself ill-treated to complain of it to someone else so as to take measures in his own defence; he would either have had to speak to someone he did not know or to someone he knew but

could not rely upon. Throughout the democratic party people approached each other suspiciously, everyone thinking that the next man had something to do with what was going on. And there were in fact among the revolutionaries some people whom no one could ever have imagined would have joined in an oligarchy. It was these who were mainly responsible for making the general mass of people so mistrustful of each other and who were of the greatest help in keeping the minority safe, since they made mutual suspicion an established thing in the popular assemblies.

If history should return to us after this eclipse, something which depends on factors still in play and thus on an outcome which no one can definitely exclude, these *Comments* may one day serve in the writing of a history of the spectacle; without any doubt the most important event to have occurred this century, and the one for which the fewest explanations have been ventured. In other circumstances, I think I could have considered myself altogether satisfied with my first work on this subject, and left others to consider future developments. But in the present situation, it seemed unlikely that anyone else would do it.

XXVIII

NETWORKS of promotion/control slide impercept-
ibly into networks of surveillance/disinformation.
Formerly one only conspired against an established
order. Today, *conspiring in its favour* is a new and flour-
ishing profession. Under spectacular domination
people conspire to maintain it, and to guarantee what
it alone would call its well-being. This conspiracy *is a
part* of its very functioning.

Provisions for a kind of preventive civil war are
already being made, adapted to variously calculated
future projections. These are the 'special squads'
responsible for local interventions according to the
needs of the integrated spectacle. Thus, for the worst
scenarios, a tactic has been planned under the name
'Three Cultures', a witty reference to a square in
Mexico City in October 1968 – though this time the
gloves would be off and the tactic applied before the
revolt occurred. Such extreme cases apart, to be a
useful tool of government unexplained assassinations
only need to be widely influential or relatively
frequent: simply knowing that they are possible
complicates calculations in many different fields. Nor
is there any need to be intelligently selective, *ad
hominem.* The entirely random application of the
procedure may well be more productive.

The composition of certain fragments of a social

critique of *rearing* has also been arranged, something which is no longer entrusted to academics or media professionals, whom it is now preferable to keep apart from excessively traditional lies in this debate: a new critique is required, advanced and exploited in a new way, controlled by another, better trained, sort of professional. In a relatively confidential manner, lucid texts are beginning to appear, anonymously, or signed by unknown authors – a tactic helped by everyone's concentration on the clowns of the spectacle, which in turn makes unknowns justly seem the most admirable – texts not only on subjects never touched on in the spectacle but also containing arguments whose force is made more striking by a calculable originality deriving from the fact that *however evident, they are never used*. This practice may serve as at least a first stage in initiation to recruit more alert intellects, who will later be told more about the possible consequences, should they seem suitable. What for some will be the first step in a career will be for others – with lower grades – the first step into the trap prepared for them.

In some cases, with issues that threaten to become controversial, another pseudo-critique can be created; and between the two opinions which will thus be put forward – both outside the impoverished conventions of the spectacle – unsophisticated judgement can oscillate indefinitely, while discussion around them can be renewed whenever necessary. Most often this concerns a general discussion of what is hidden by the media, and this discussion can be strongly critical, and on some points quite evidently intelligent, yet always curiously decentred. Topics and words have been artificially chosen, with the aid of computers programmed in critical thought. These texts always contain certain gaps, which are quite hard to spot but nonetheless remarkable: the vanishing point of perspective is always abnormally absent. They resemble those *facsimiles* of famous weapons, which only lack the firing-pin. This is inevitably a *lateral critique*, which perceives many things with considerable candour and accuracy, but places itself to one side. Not because it affects some sort of impartiality, for on the contrary it must seem to find much fault, yet without ever apparently feeling the need to reveal its *cause*, to state, even implicitly, where it is coming from and where it wants to go.

To this kind of counter-journalistic false critique can be added the organised practice of *rumour* which we know to be originally a sort of uncontrollable by-product of spectacular information, since everyone, however vaguely, perceives something misleading about the latter and trust it as little as it deserves. Rumour began as something superstitious, naïve, self-deluding. More recently, however, surveillance has begun introducing into the population people capable of starting rumours which suit it at the very first signal. It has been decided here to apply in practice the observations of a theory formulated some thirty years ago, whose origins lie in American sociology of advertising – the theory of individuals known as 'pacemakers', that is, those whom others in their milieu come to follow and imitate – but this time moving from spontaneity to control. Budgetary, or extra-budgetary, means have also been released to fund numerous auxiliaries; beside the former specialists of the recent past, academics and media professionals, sociologists and police. To believe in the continuing mechanical application of past models leads to just as many errors as the general ignorance of the past. 'Rome is no longer in Rome', and the Mafia are no longer thieves. And the surveillance and disinformation services are as far removed from the police and informers of former times – for example, from the *roussins* and *mouchards* of the Second Empire – as the present special services in all countries are from the officers of the army general staff's *Deuxième Bureau* in 1914.

Since art is dead, it has evidently become extremely easy to disguise police as artists. When the latest imitations of a recuperated neo-dadaism are allowed to pontificate proudly in the media, and thus also to tinker with the décor of official palaces, like court jesters to the kings of junk, it is evident that by the same process a cultural cover is guaranteed for every agent or auxiliary of the state's networks of persuasion. Empty pseudo-museums, or pseudo-research centres on the work of nonexistent personalities, can be opened just as fast as reputations are made for journalist-cops, historian-cops, or novelist-cops. No doubt Arthur Cravan foresaw this world when he wrote in *Maintenant*: 'Soon we will only see artists in the streets, and it will take no end of effort to find a single man.' This is indeed the sense of the revived form of an old quip of Parisian loafers: 'Hello there, artists! Too bad if I've got it wrong.'

Things having become what they are, we can now witness the use of collective authorship by the most modern publishing houses, that is to say, the ones with the best commercial distribution. Since their pseudonyms are only authenticated by the newspapers, they can swop them around, collaborate, replace each other, take on new artificial brains. Their task is to express the ideas and lifestyles of the epoch, not because of their personalities, but because they are ordered to. Those who believe that they are truly independent, individual literary entrepreneurs can knowingly vouch for the fact that Ducasse has had a row with the Comte de Lautréamont, that Dumas isn't Maquet, that we must never confuse Erckmann with Chatrian; that Censier and Daubenton are no longer on speaking terms. It might be best to say that this type of modern author was a follower of Rimbaud, at least in so far as 'I is someone else.'

The whole history of spectacular society called for the secret services to play the pivotal role; for it is in them that the features and force of such a society are concentrated to the highest degree. Moreover they are always also the arbiters of that society's general interests, despite their modest title of 'services'. There is no corruption here, for they faithfully express the common morals of the spectacular century. Thus do watchers and watched sail forth on a boundless ocean. The spectacle has brought the secret to victory, and must be more and more controlled by *specialists in secrecy* who are certainly not only officials who have to different degrees managed to free themselves from state control; who are not only officials.

XXIX

A GENERAL working rule of the integrated spectacle, at least for those who manage its affairs, is that in this framework, *everything which can be done, must be done.* This means that every new instrument must be employed, whatever the cost. New machinery everywhere becomes the goal and the driving force of the system, and is the only thing which can significantly modify its progress, every time its use is imposed without further reflection. Society's owners indeed want above all to keep a certain 'social relation between people', but they must also maintain continual technological innovation; for that was one of the obligations that came with their inheritance. This law must also thus apply to the services which safeguard domination. When an instrument has been perfected it must be used, and its use will reinforce the very conditions that favour this use. Thus it is that emergency procedures become standard procedures.

In a certain sense the coherence of spectacular society proves revolutionaries right, since it is evident that one cannot reform the most trifling detail without taking the whole thing apart. But at the same time this coherence has eliminated every organised revolutionary tendency by eliminating those social terrains where it had more or less effectively been able to find expression: from trade unions to newspapers, towns to books. In a single movement, it has been possible to illuminate the incompetence and thought-lessness of which this tendency was quite naturally the bearer. And on an individual level, the reigning coherence is quite capable of eliminating, or buying off such exceptions as may arise.

XXX

SURVEILLANCE would be much more dangerous had it not been led by its ambition for absolute control of everything to a point where it encountered difficulties created by its own progress. There is a contradiction between the mass of information collected on a growing number of individuals, and the time and intelligence available to analyse it, not to mention its actual interest. The quantity of data demands constant summarising: much of it will be lost, and what remains is still too long to be read. Management of surveillance and manipulation is uncoordinated. Indeed there is a widespread struggle for a share of the profits, and thus also for favouring the development of this or that potential in the existing society, to the detriment of the other potentials, which nonetheless, so long as they are all tarred with the same brush, are considered equally respectable.

This struggle is also a game. Each control comes to over-value his agents, as well as his opponents. Each country, not to mention the numerous supranational alliances, currently possesses an indefinite number of police and counter-espionage services, along with secret services, both state and para-state. There are also many private companies dealing in surveillance, security and investigation. The large multinationals naturally have their own services; but so do nationalised companies, even those of modest scale, which will still pursue independent policies at a national and sometimes an international level. A nuclear power group will fight against an oil group, even though both are owned by the same state and what is more are dialectically united by their interest in maintaining high oil prices on the world market. Each particular industry's security service combats the threat of sabotage, while organising it, when necessary, against their rivals: a company with important interests in undersea tunnels will be favourably disposed to the hazards of ferries and may bribe newspapers in financial trouble to ensure they spot these hazards without delay and without too much reflection; a company competing with Sandoz will be indifferent to underground springs in the Rhine valley. Secrets are subject to secret surveillance. Thus each of these organisations, all subtly united around the executives of *raison d'État*, aspires to its own private hegemony of meaning. For meaning has been lost along with an identifiable centre.

Going from success to success, until 1968 modern society was convinced it was loved. It has since had to abandon these dreams; it prefers to be feared. It knows full well that 'its innocent air has gone forever'.

So it is that thousands of plots in favour of the established order tangle and clash almost everywhere, as the overlap of secret networks and secret issues or activities grows ever more dense along with their rapid integration into every sector of economics, politics and culture. In all areas of social life the degree of intermingling in surveillance, disinformation and security activities gets greater and greater. The plot having thickened to the point where it is almost out in the open, each part of it now starts to interfere with, or worry, the others, for all these professional conspirators are spying on each other without really knowing why, are colliding by chance yet not identifying each other with any certainty. Who is observing whom? On whose behalf, apparently? And actually? The real influences remain hidden, and the ultimate aims can barely be suspected and almost never understood. So that while no one can be sure he is not being tricked or manipulated, it is rare for the string-puller to know he has succeeded. And in any case, to be on the winning side of manipulation does not mean that one has chosen the right strategic perspective. Tactical successes can thus lead great powers down dangerous roads.

In the same network and apparently pursuing similar goals, those who are only a part of the network are necessarily ignorant of the hypotheses and conclusions of the other parts, and above all of their controlling nucleus. The reasonably well known fact that all information on whatever subject under observation may well be entirely imaginary, or seriously falsified, or very inadequately interpreted, complicates and undermines to a great degree the calculations of the inquisitors. For what is sufficient to condemn someone is far less sure when it comes to recognising or using him. Since sources of information are in competition, so are falsifications.

It is in these circumstances that we can speak of domination's falling rate of profit, as it spreads to almost the whole of social space and consequently increases both its personnel and its means. For now each means aspires, and labours, to become an end. Surveillance spies on itself, and plots against itself.

Its principal present contradiction, finally, is that it is spying on, infiltrating and pressurising *an absent entity*: that which is supposed to be trying to subvert the social order. But where can it actually be seen at work? Certainly conditions have never been so seriously revolutionary, but it is only governments who think so. Negation has been so thoroughly deprived of its thought that it was dispersed long ago. Because of this it remains only a vague, yet highly disturbing threat, and surveillance in its turn has been deprived of its preferred field of activity. Surveillance and intervention are thus rightly led by the present exigencies determining their terms of engagement to operate on the very terrain of this threat in order to combat it *in advance*. This is why surveillance has an interest in organising poles of negation itself, which it can instruct with more than the discredited means of the spectacle, so as to manipulate, not terrorists this time, but theories.

XXXI

BALTASAR Gracián, that great authority on historical time, tells us with considerable pertinency in *The Courtier*: 'Be it words or action, all must be measured by time. We must choose when we are able; for time and tide wait on no man.' But Omar Khayyám was less of an optimist: 'We are the puppets and the firmament is the puppet-master,/In actual fact and not as a metaphor,/For a time we acted on this stage,/We went back one by one into the box of oblivion.'

XXXII

THE French Revolution brought great changes in the art of war. It was from that experience that Clausewitz could draw the distinction between tactics, as the use of forces in battle to obtain victory, and strategy, as the use of victories in battle to attain the goals of a war. Europe was subjugated, quickly and lastingly, by the results. But the theory was not proven till later, and was developed unevenly. First to be appreciated were the positive features directly brought about by a profound social transformation: the enthusiasm and mobility of a greatly enlarged army which lived off the land and was relatively independent of stores and supply trains. Such useful elements were soon counterbalanced by the appearance on the enemy side of similar elements: in Spain the French armies encountered an equal popular enthusiasm; in the vast spaces of Russia, a land they could not live off; after the rising in Germany, numerically far superior forces. However the effect of a total break, in the new French tactics, which was the simple basis on which Bonaparte founded his strategy – the latter consisting of using victories *in advance,* as if acquired on credit to understand manoeuvres in all their diverse variants from the start as consequences of a victory which while not yet obtained would certainly be at the first onslaught – derived also from the forced abandonment of false ideas.

These tactics demanded an abrupt break from these false ideas, and at the same time, by the concomitant play of the other innovations outlined above, found the means to achieve such a break. The newly mustered French soldiers were incapable of fighting in line, that is, of keeping ranks and firing on command. They would thus be deployed in extended order, firing at will as they advanced on the enemy. Now in fact independent fire was shown to be the only effective kind, a genuinely destructive use of musketry which proved the most decisive factor in military engagements of the period. Yet military thinking had universally rejected this conclusion in the century that was ending, and indeed debate on the issue continued through most of the new century, despite constant practical demonstration in battle, and the ceaseless progress in range and rate of fire.

Similarly, the establishment of spectacular domination is such a profound social transformation that it has radically altered the art of government. This simplification, which has quickly borne such fruit in practice, has yet to be fully comprehended in theory. Old prejudices everywhere belied, precautions now useless, and even the residues of scruples from an earlier age, still clog up the thinking of quite a number of rulers, preventing them from recognising something which practice demonstrates and proves every single day. Not only are the subjected led to believe that to all intents and purposes they are still living in a world which in fact has been eliminated, but the rulers themselves sometimes suffer from the absurd belief that in some respects they do too. They come to believe in a part of what they have suppressed, as if it remained a reality and had still to be included in their calculations. This backwardness will not last long. Those who have achieved so much so easily must necessarily go further. It should not be thought that those who have been too slow to appreciate the pliability of the new rules of their game and its form of barbaric grandeur, will last forever like some archaism in proximity to real power. It is certainly not the spectacle's destiny to end up as enlightened despotism.

We must conclude that a changeover is imminent and ineluctable in the coopted cast who serve the interests of domination, and above all manage the protection of that domination. In such an affair, innovation will surely not be displayed on the spectacle's stage. It appears instead like lightning, which we know only when it strikes. This changeover, which will conclude decisively the work of these spectacular times, will occur discreetly, and conspiratorially, even though it concerns those within the inner circles of power. It will select those who will share this central exigency: that they clearly see what obstacles they have overcome, and of what they are capable.

XXXIII

THE same Sardou also wrote:

Vainly relates to the subject; *in vain* to the object; *uselessly* simply means with no use for anyone. One has worked *vainly* when one has done so without success, so that one has wasted one's time and effort: one has worked *in vain* when one has done so without achieving the intended result, because of the defectiveness of the work. If I cannot succeed in completing a piece of work, I am working *vainly*; I am uselessly wasting my time and effort. If the work I have done does not have the result I was expecting, if I have not attained my goal, I have worked *in vain*; that is to say, I have done something useless....

It is also said that someone has worked *vainly* when he has not been rewarded for his work, or when this work has not been approved; for in this case the worker has wasted his time and effort, without this prejudicing in any way the value of his work, which indeed may be very good.

Paris, February–April 1988

TRANSLATOR'S NOTES

The French edition of *Comments* has no footnotes, and it would have been inappropriate to add any to this translation. However, with the author's approval, I have included these brief notes on certain references and allusions that might otherwise remain *unnecessarily* obscure to English readers.

Page vi   Sun Tzu. Guy Debord's epigraph is taken from the first European translation of *The Art of War*, by the Jesuit J.J.L. Amiot (1782). The best available English translation, by Samuel B. Griffith (Oxford 1963), does not include this passage, so I have had to translate from the French.

Page 17   '... wine experts able to con connoisseurs into admiring their new, more distinctive, flavours.' The French here is '... des experts en vins qui entraîneront les *caves* à aimer leurs nouveaux parfums, plus reconnaissables.' Debord's pun on the two meanings of *caves* – wine–cellars (fem.) and hopeless dupes or suckers (masc.) – is unfortunately lost in English. The word's underworld etymology is instructive. It originally referred to anyone who worked in a legitimate job; hence to someone who did not know how to live; and hence to any kind of dupe.

Page 17 '... under a poor cloak you commonly find a good drinker.' The proverb is from *Don Quixote*, quoted by the Duchess in her conversation with Sancho Panza (vol. II, book 3, ch. 1). The Spanish is, 'Debajo de mala capa, suele haber buen bebedor.' I have used the Samuel Putnam translation.

Page 20 '... *men resemble their times more than their fathers.*' An Arab proverb, dating from the fourteenth century.

Page 29 'They are jeering at us, and we know whom these programmes are for.' The French here is, 'On nous siffle, et l'on sait pour qui sont ces structures.' Debord is playing on a famous line from Racine's *Andromache*, Act V, Scene 3: 'Pour qui sont ces serpents qui sifflent sur vos têtes?'

Page 33 Dr Archambeau. In 1984, seemingly motivated by professional jealousy, certain colleagues of a Dr Archambeau at a hospital in Poitiers caused the death of some of his patients in the operating-theatre by reversing the oxygen and nitrogen supplies during resuscitation. Archambeau was eventually acquitted of any blame, but the real culprits were never discovered.

Page 39 It was Marx who defined political economy as 'the final denial of humanity'.

Page 41 '... *illusionists, barkers and stool-pigeons* ...' The French here is 'illusionnistes, aboyeurs et barons'. *Baron*, a word still in common use, refers to a trickster's accomplice, planted in the crowd, who helps to dupe others either by raising objections which the trickster can easily refute, or by pretending to buy whatever is on offer. This was also the nineteenth-century meaning of 'stool-pigeon', although the word is now used in a different sense. I cannot find a modern English equivalent, though some American meanings of 'stooge' might be adequate.

Page 42   '... rather in the way that the one who was waiting for Grouchy instead saw Blücher join the battle, it was simply a matter of calling in the Guard of experts.' The battle is Waterloo, the 'one', Napoleon. The allusion is to Victor Hugo's description of Waterloo in his poem 'L'Expiation': seeing the battle was going badly for the French, Napoleon summoned the Imperial Guard to enter the fray.

Page 54   'GAL'. Grupo Anti-Terorista de Liberación.

Page 55   "the mad killers of Brabant". *Les tueurs fous de Brabant* was the media's name for the perpetrators of a series of murders in Belgium in the 1980s. The murders were carried out during a number of raids on supermarkets: on each occasion the gang, armed with military weapons, shot six or seven people, apparently at random, and stole very small amounts of money. Recent newspaper revelations have suggested that the choice of victims may not have been entirely random, and that the murderers may have been linked to right-wing organisations.

Page 55   '... home is the pirate, home from the sea ...' The allusion is to Robert Louis Stevenson's 'Requiem'. But some of the references here are more specific. Debord has pointed out that 'the thief who no longer needs to steal', for example, was François Besse, the former accomplice of Jacques Mesrine, who has disappeared without trace.

Pages 67–68   Jaurès was assassinated in the Chope du Croissant (now the Café Chope du Croissant), 146 rue Montmartre, on 31 July 1914.

Page 74   '… under the name "Three Cultures" …' On 2 October 1968, police opened fire on student demonstrators in Plaza de las Tres Culturas in Mexico City, killing many. During the preceding fortnight, at least fifty more students had been killed during police attacks on strike meetings and the university campus.

Page 77   'Rome is no longer in Rome …' The quotation is from a line in Racine's *Mithridate*: 'Rome n'est plus dans Rome; elle est toute où je suis.'

Page 78   'Hello there, artists …' The French is, 'Salut, les artistes! Tant pis si je me trompes.' The old low-life greeting was, 'Salut, les hommes …': Debord has substituted 'artists' for 'men'.

Page 78   'Ducasse has had a row with the Comte de Lautréamont …' Isidor Ducasse was of course the Comte de Lautréamont. Auguste Macquet (or Maquet), a historian, was one of Dumas Père's chief literary collaborators. Emile Erckmann and Alexandre Chatrian (1822–99 and 1826–90) wrote several novels and plays together over some forty years, many of them set in their native Alsace. Censier-Daubenton is a Paris Métro station.

Page 82   'Its innocent air has gone forever.' Debord is quoting from his film, *In girum imus nocte et consumimur igni.*

I would like to thank Guy Debord, Liz Heron and Martin Thom for their help with this translation.

MI

Radical Thinkers ▼

Printed in the United States
by Baker & Taylor Publisher Services